IMAGES
of America

# U.S. NAVY SEALs
# IN SAN DIEGO

SEAL is an acronym for sea, air, and land. In this photograph, SEAL and UDT (Underwater Demolition Team) members of the navy's Leap Frogs jump team demonstrate an aerial star formation as they parachute above the U.S. Naval Amphibious Base (NAB), Coronado, San Diego Bay. (Courtesy C. Maury.)

**ON THE COVER:** A UDT-3 sling-man leans over the tube of the rubber boat with a hoop sling, placing the hoop over the arm of a Frogman; wearing a rubber suit and using boat speed, momentum, and hoop sling elastics, he pulls the Frogman into the inflatable boat small (IBS). The UDT-3-1 landing craft personnel reconnaissance (LCPR) boat speeds by to conduct drop and pickup training off the coast of the Silver Strand in Coronado, California, on September 24, 1949. From left to right are Lt. Gordon Trible, Tex Modesett, and Lt. Peter Hustad. (Courtesy Commander Naval Special Warfare Command [CNSWC] historian.)

IMAGES
*of America*

# U.S. NAVY SEALS
# IN SAN DIEGO

Michael P. Wood

ARCADIA
PUBLISHING

Published by Arcadia Publishing
Charleston, South Carolina

Printed in the United States of America

Library of Congress Control Number: 2008941503

For all general information contact Arcadia Publishing at:
Telephone 843-853-2070
Fax 843-853-0044
E-mail sales@arcadiapublishing.com
For customer service and orders:
Toll-Free 1-888-313-2665

Visit us on the Internet at www.arcadiapublishing.com

*To all the Frogs and SEALs of the past, present, and future where your service has contributed to the freedoms we all enjoy today. Wherever or whenever you served, we are all part of the same team; it is all the "Same Blood just Different Mud."*

# CONTENTS

# ACKNOWLEDGMENTS

First and foremost, I would like to thank all of the current, retired, and former Frogs and SEALs for their dedicated service to this country. Their service and accomplishments are inspirational for this and many generations to come. So thank you for your dedication, which these photographs and stories represent. There are many of those individual Frogs and SEALs who helped with this book whether in providing photographs, historical background, or historical editing. A representative few to thank are Roger Cook, Ken Garrett, Chip Maury, Don Rose, Jerry Todd, Bob Kelley, Steve Robinson, Walt Otte, Lou De Lara, Lee Hughs, Phil Carrico, Frank Toms, Mack Boyton, and others of the Fifties Frogs organization.

Key to the development of a book like this is the access to historical photographs and the relevant information. Members of the National Navy UDT-SEAL Museum in Fort Pierce, Florida, and the historian's office at Naval Special Warfare Command (NSWC) in Coronado, California, were the providers of the majority of these historical photographs. Many thanks belong to Mike Howard, director, and Ruth McSwean, curator, of the UDT-SEAL Museum for letting me have access to their multitude of electronic and print photograph files. Special thanks also go to Roger Clapp, command historian at NSWC for the historical photograph access but also for his invaluable advice on organizing the book and leads to the specific historical data of the various UDT and SEAL command histories. Most important is my thanks to my wife, Joyce, for her patience while a book widow and understanding during the many hours I spent hours researching and developing this book. Dear, your editorial support was especially helpful!

I would also like to acknowledge a special group of men and women who were and are essential to the success of Naval Special Warfare (NSW) throughout the years. These are the members of the Special Boat Teams, Units, and Coastal River Squadrons and today's Special Warfare Combatant Crewmen. Their NSW support and service is not covered in this history book of San Diego Frogs and SEALs only because of the relatively small content size of this regional history book. Your story is worthy of a book all by itself.

All photographs used in this book come from the archives of the NSWC historian, unless otherwise noted.

# INTRODUCTION

To meet the need for a beach reconnaissance force, selected army and navy personnel were assembled on the East Coast at NAB Little Creek, Virginia, in August 1942, later to see combat in November 1942 during the first Allied landings in Europe, in North Africa, Italy, and France. But it was November 23, 1943, at the Gilbert Islands Tarawa Beaches, where tension was high with the multitude of amphibious landing craft noise droning and waves crashing on the beach, that the marines prepared to go ashore during the World War II amphibious operations. Suddenly, many of the landing craft ground to a halt many yards short of the beach, running aground on unforeseen and unreported shoals and coral heads, forcing the heavily laden marines to enter much deeper water than anticipated. Many marines drowned that day, and thus was born the requirement in the Pacific for some type of waterman to survey near shore waters and beaches prior to future amphibious operations.

These watermen were called many names early on, from Scouts and Raiders to Naval Combat Demolition Units, Office of Strategic Service Operational Swimmers, and finally Underwater Demolition Teams, and they were later known and memorialized as Frogmen. The Frogmen had to be able to do many things with very little equipment and very little protection. They had to be able to swim long distances, withstand cold water for long periods of time, conduct maritime reconnaissance and surveillance sometimes under heavy gunfire while cold and exhausted, and still keep accurate records to produce detailed landing charts at the end of the mission.

This took a very special type of person and a special type of training program to produce that waterman. Thus was born Basic Underwater Demolition and SEAL training (BUD/S). Although BUD/S was known by a couple of other names early on and the length of the training changed through the years, the essence of the training has remained the same throughout. The goal is to break the tadpoles ("newbie" Frogmen) down, rebuild them, severely test them, and once proven, teach them to be warriors above and below the water, and finally teach them the current tactics, weapons, explosives, and technologies of the day. What makes BUD/S different from any other military training program even today is the severe testing, which proves to those who make it that they are capable of 10 times more than they realize. Today that severe test is known as Hell Week and is named appropriately.

The personal experiences may have varied, but basically Hell Week means staying awake, alert, and functional for six to seven days and five to six nights without any sleep while conducting non-stop evolutions of running, swimming, paddling boats, and exercising. It is during this period when most who decide to quit do so in the first two days. Due to sleep deprivation, those who make it this far in Hell Week, to the second or third night, experience strange sensory illusions while wide awake that are dream-like, something that they have never experienced before in their lives. By the third night without sleep, hallucinations begin to expose the tired and worn tadpole to visions of the wildest imaginations. Hell Week provides these tadpoles the self-confidence from deep within and ingrains in them as an individual and as a team that they can accomplish almost anything they set their minds to do. This may be perceived by others as cockiness, bravado, or ego, but for the most part, it is a quiet confidence that is unshakable. The Frogmen of waters and beaches of World War II and the SEALs from the caves and deserts of Afghanistan and Iraq are all of the same mold.

In 1962, President Kennedy sought more navy unconventional forces to add to the capabilities of the UDTs, which formed the beginnings of the sea, air, and land (or SEAL) teams. These SEAL teams added to their already impressive training and skill sets more advanced training that included parachute training, jungle warfare, small unit tactics, intelligence collection, and working with indigenous fighters. The strength of the SEALs is not so much their training, doctrine, weapons, or tactics but their ability to adapt to the ever-changing warfare requirements. In Vietnam, SEALs adapted and used the Vietcong's own way of jungle operations against them but added nighttime guerilla tactics to terrorize the VC. In Afghanistan, they adapted to mountainous and cave tactics, and in Iraq, they mastered and adapted urban operations. SEALs weapons, tactics, communications, and technologies continuously adapt to the changing warfare requirements.

There is another group of NSW operators that are relatively unknown and are descendants of both UDT and SEAL teams; today they form SEAL delivery vehicle (SDV) teams. SDVs are wet submersibles used to transport SEALs and, at one time, were used by both the UDT and SEAL teams but later were formed into their own special teams of underwater warriors. SDVs were used in Vietnam by SEAL Team ONE (ST-1) for a POW rescue mission in Haiphong Harbor, but by the time of SDV operations during Desert Storm, SDV teams had been formed. SEAL Delivery Vehicle Team ONE (SDVT-1) was based in Coronado. This command operated the SDV, a deep submergence system known as Dry Deck Shelter (DDS) that attaches to the hull of fast attack and ballistic missile submarines, and later the advanced SEAL delivery vehicle, a dry submersible. SDV operators are also well trained in land warfare operations, usually conducting sniper or reconnaissance and surveillance operations.

After Vietnam, many West Coast SEALs returned from the war and were drafted into working with another type of seal, of the marine mammal type. They became members of Inshore Undersea Warfare Group ONE (IUWG-1), an NSW command, and trained both dolphins and California sea lions in marine mammal programs known as Project Quick Find and Project Short Time. The SEALs of Project Quick Find were well publicized in their work of training sea lions to dive and mark inert war reserve anti-submarine rocket (ASROC) missiles on the ocean floor for recovery. These SEALs were trained in animal behavioral psychology and participated in sea lion captures at San Nicholas Island, California, under the guidelines of the Marine Mammal Protection Act. SEALs' involvement continued with the evolved navy's marine mammal program, expanding the program into mine search and recovery.

Today U.S. Navy SEALs are stationed worldwide, and many of the new recruits learned their skills at the Naval Amphibious Base in San Diego, California. Here they learned the basics as well as advanced tactics, techniques, and procedures of UDT and SEAL operations. Since 1943, U.S. Navy SEALs and Frogmen have been stationed here and some have remained, calling San Diego their home. Many others have gone on to achieve even greater accomplishments both inside and outside the NSW community.

This book will serve as a mere sampling of the SEAL and Frogman warrior history. It is by no means all inclusive, and there will be many more stories that still need to be told.

# One

# UNDERWATER

# DEMOLITION TEAMS

In 1943, the Amphibious Training Base (ATB) Coronado began operations. In 1946, Frogman teams were reduced from 30 to 6 UDTs: Able, Baker, Charlie, Dog, Echo, and Foxtrot, consisting of four officers and 50 enlisted. By mid-1946, four alphabet teams were redesignated numbered teams UDT 1, 2, 3, and 4, with 1 and 3 assigned to Commander Amphibious Pacific at ATB Coronado. UDT-1 was stationed in San Diego on May 21, 1946, before the Korean War, and UDT-3 was established on May 5, 1951. Their beginnings were humble, living in tents and then Quonset huts both on the bay side of NAB and later on the ocean side of the Silver Strand. UDT-5 was assembled at Fort Pierce, Florida, in January 1944 and in February moved to a demolition base on Maui for formal commissioning under the command of Lt. Cdr. D. L. Kauffman.

In February and March 1954, UDT 1, 3, and 5 were redesignated, with UDT-1 becoming UDT-11 and UDT-3 becoming UDT-12; UDT-5 was decommissioned and UDT-13 was formed. On August 10, 1959, UDU-1 (Underwater Demolition Unit), UDT-11, and UDT-12 moved from the humble half-round Quonset huts to a more permanent building that is still used today. It was this UDT compound where they were home based and rotated in and out of for service in the Vietnam War and later conflicts. The three UDTs were active participants in their communities throughout San Diego County by participating in demonstrations, community service, and parades in Coronado and San Diego. In June 1971, UDT-13 was decommissioned. The UDTs era came to an end about May 1983, when UDT-11 became SEAL Team FIVE (ST-5) and UDT-12 was redesignated SDVT-1.

UDTs are well known for their service during World War II, Korea, and Vietnam. Their exploits were made famous in movies and television, such as the *The Frogmen* movie with Richard Widmark and the *Sea Hunt* television series with Lloyd Bridges. Many Coronado Frogmen served as extras or advisors for both. UDTs of this period also participated in many other significant events, such as space capsule recoveries for all the Apollo missions and Skylab missions, special electronics testing, new diving equipment testing, Arctic expeditions supporting the distance early warning (DEW) line, and defense of Taiwan preparations.

UDT Petty Officer, Third Class, Hopper readies his Churchill fins and face mask for Balikpapan landing operations. The Battle of Balikpapan was the concluding stage of the Borneo campaign (1945). The landings took place on July 1, 1945. The UDTs of this era were truly the naked warriors, as evidenced by this photograph.

UDT Frogmen loaded up in LCPRs from the USS *Clemson* APD-3 transit toward the beach during the Saipan landing on the Mariana Islands on July 13, 1944.

After World War II and before the Korean Conflict, UDTs in Coronado, California, conducted drop and pickup training on the ocean side of the Silver Strand. The cast-master, wearing a helmet, gives the arm signal for the dry-suit-wearing Frogman to cast off of the IBS as the LCPR is underway at high speed. Below, the hoop-man extends the hoop out over the IBS tube so the Frogman in the water with his arm up can be picked up into the speeding boat. The Silver Strand coastline is in the background.

The *San Diego Union* newspaper's August 16, 1950, headline reports, "Navy Commandos Cripple Rail Line." The article continues, stating, "U.S. navy commandos in a daring raid have crippled the Korean Communists' main rail supply line by sneaking ashore from a warship and dynamiting a tunnel less than 100 miles from the Russian border." A military spokesman described the size of the party as "more than a demolition team." The tunnel, which was blasted sky high, was just a few miles from Chong-jin, an iron and steel producing center with a population of 250,000.

UDT Frogmen study the situation prior to destroying a North Korean minefield during the Wonson invasion in October 1950. (Courtesy National Archives.)

UDT personnel paddle their rubber boat ashore through Wonson Harbor, en route to explode North Korean mines on October 25, 1950. (Courtesy National Archives.)

A UDT Frogman free dives down to tie a right-hand knot from the demolition pack to the explosive detonation cord trunk line for a simultaneous detonation of many demolitions packs in the waters of Saipan.

UDT-1 First platoon is in the foreground, and other UDT-3 Frogmen conduct training at Nagia Beach near Camp McGill 7 miles from Yokosuka while waiting to go to Korea. From left to right are Dick Bereton, Don Rose, Ken Garret, Travis Lane, Dan Fulton, and Acton Johnson. (Courtesy D. Rose.)

Premier "Frogman", Coronado Calif. - 1951

In May 1951, Widmark Studio gave a pre-showing of the movie *The Frogmen* in the NAB Coronado Theater for UDT-1 and selected new UDT trainees. Afterward the studio hosted a party and dance. Sn. Ken Garrett remembers, "Mr. Widmark approached our booth and asked 'Would you fellas mind if I sat down?' True to Frog fashion, Shep Sheppard gruffly answered 'Why not, you bought the beer.'" From left to right are Richard Widmark, Jack Molden, Robert ("Shep") Sheppard, Ken Garrett, Paul Brewton, Howard Whitfield, and Lt. Cdr. David F. "Kelly" Welch. (Courtesy K. Garrett.)

At right is actor Lloyd Bridges as Mike Nelson from the television series *Sea Hunt*. *The Frogmen* movie and the television show *Sea Hunt* inspired many young men of the 1950s to 1970s to become Frogmen and to try out for UDT training. Lou Delara and other UDT-1 frogs of the time assisted Lloyd Bridges in scuba dive training and served as extras in the early *Sea Hunt* shows.

15

Walt Otte, UDT-1 First platoon, and his Alaskan helper hold onto the swimmer line reel while the platoon conducts a hydrographic reconnaissance to support a resupply mission for the distant early warning (DEW) line in Alaska in 1957. UDTs also conducted ice and obstacle demolitions. (Courtesy W. Otte.)

UDT-12 Frogmen surface from the bottom after gathering survey findings in support of an Arctic expedition in resupplying the DEW line.

UDT Frogmen used a unique method of floating assembled sections of MK-8 hose demolitions on air mattresses during submarine dam destruction operations in Dinh Tuong Province, Vietnam. Once the explosive hose was positioned correctly, it was then sunk in place and cratering charges added. Battling current, waist-deep mud, and chest-deep water, the Frogmen worked for days on each dam. With each blast, tons of mud, water, and foliage were sent several hundred feet skyward—removing all traces of the dam.

UDT-11 Frogmen ready an inflatable boat beside an Apollo 14 Command Module mock-up surrounded by its flotation collar during a practice recovery mission at San Diego Bay in December 1970.

UDU-1 Frogmen ready a training capsule for helicopter lift into San Diego Bay. Frogmen are wearing standard-issue UDT life jackets and shorts and carrying K-bar knives and duck-feet fins. There were 11 Apollo missions, including Apollos 11–17, and at least three Skylab missions in which UDT Frogmen played a role in space capsule recovery.

One UDT-11 Frogman opens the hatch as the other stands by on the flotation collar ready to help the Apollo 15 astronauts exit the space capsule with the USS *Okinawa*, LPH3, in the background. At left is Fred Schmidt, and at right is Jerry Todd. Below, the UDT-11 Frogman fully opens the capsule hatch as one of the astronauts looks out in anticipation. Inside the capsule is astronaut David Scott, and opening the hatch is Fred Schmidt. (Both, courtesy J. Todd.)

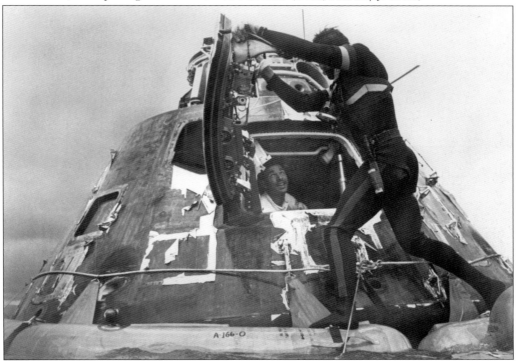

A UDT-12 Second platoon Frogman, Alan Odell, writes depth soundings on a plastic slate strapped to his forearm while conducting an administrative parallel reconnaissance of a beach in the Philippine Islands. The lead line wrapped around his hand was used for taking the depth soundings. (Author's collection.)

UDT-12 Second platoon Frogmen form the beach party that holds the range flags and flutter board line on the beach. The range flags help swimmers in the water line up in a straight line, and the flutter board line keeps the swimmers separated at 25-yard intervals. They are conducting an administrative parallel hydrographic reconnaissance of a beach in the Philippine Islands in 1982. (Author's collection.)

Two UDT-12 Frogmen diving with MK-15 underwater breathing apparatus (UBA) conduct an underwater hydrographic reconnaissance using a fishing reel line to maintain equal 25-yard distance between lanes. The attack board compass was used to maintain the same direction for their perpendicular lanes to the beach, and the depth gauge was used to take depth soundings. The MK-15 UBA is a diving rig that maintains a constant partial pressure of oxygen ($O_2$). (Author's collection.)

UDT-12 Frogmen diving the MK-6 mixed-gas rebreather conduct the same fishing reel tactics for an underwater hydrographic reconnaissance. The MK-6 rebreather oxygen ratio is controlled manually by the diver and is the predecessor to the MK-15 UBA above. (Author's collection.)

Members of UDT-12 Second platoon take a break from reconnaissance and demolitions while on a Western Pacific deployment to enjoy a waterfall shower at Talofofo Falls in Guam. UDT platoons in this time period had up to 21 men in the platoon, ensuring enough personnel for hydrographic reconnaissance. (Author's collection.)

The author, Michael P. Wood, serving as the UDT-12 Second platoon assistant platoon commander (AOIC), conducts rappelling training down into the well deck of the USS *Cayuga*, LST-1186, while on deployment in the Western Pacific. (Author's collection.)

# Two

# SEAL TEAMS

The requirement for the navy's unconventional warriors, Navy SEALs, is credited to Pres. John F. Kennedy in a speech he gave to Congress. The development of this navy unconventional warfare capability though was the idea of and emerged in outline form on March 10, 1961, by the Strategic Plans Division, who then forwarded the proposal to the Chief of Naval Operations before it filtered up through the chain of command to President Kennedy.

On January 1, 1962, the West Coast SEAL Team ONE (ST-1) was commissioned at the Naval Amphibious Base in Coronado, California. This occurred a few days prior to the commissioning of SEAL Team TWO (ST-2) on the East Coast, providing ST-1 the distinction of being the first SEAL team. There is still raucous debate today about this "who is first" distinction. What is undebatable is that the SEAL mission was to conduct counter guerilla warfare and clandestine operations in maritime and riverine environments. SEALs immediately deployed to Vietnam to operate in the deltas, rivers, and canals of Vietnam and effectively disrupted the enemy's maritime lines of communication. The enemy quickly felt the SEAL presence and awarded another name for these unconventional warriors: "the men with green faces." SEALs initially advised and trained Vietnamese forces but were soon conducting nighttime direct action missions, ambushes, and raids to capture prisoners of high intelligence value. SEAL teams began their operational reputation in the jungles of Vietnam, and from March 1967 to December 1971, ST-1 sent 39 SEAL platoons to fight the Vietcong and North Vietnamese.

Naval Operations Support Group was also established the same year as ST-1 to provide operational control of the UDT and SEAL teams as well as the Boat and Beach Jumper units. ST-1 served as the only West Coast SEAL team for over 20 years until the formation of SEAL Team THREE (ST-3) on October 1, 1983, and ST-5, formerly UDT-11, on May 1, 1983. A major command change occurred in March 1988 when operational control of Naval Special Warfare Groups ONE (NSWG-1) and TWO (NSWG-2) was transferred from the commander-in-chief's Pacific and Atlantic Fleet to CNSWC in Coronado, California. SEAL Team SEVEN (ST-7) commissioning followed 13 years later on March 17, 2002, quadrupling the SEAL command growth in San Diego.

ST-1 platoon, the first NSW group to Nha Be in 1965, poses next to Mighty Mo LCM-6. Early SEAL platoons bought their own camouflage uniforms and berets from Sears, or they appropriated Tiger Stripe cammies from the army. From left to right are (first row) Maynard Weyers, ? Rascheck, Billy Machen, Chuck Stenners, Van Orden, ? Wilcox, ? Cline, Ron Bell, and Tom Truxell; (second row) Lieutenant Tomsho, Lieutenant Pechacek, Roger Mascone, ? Parsons, ? Suazo, A. J. Smith, John Campbell, Jim Pahia, Ted Mathison, Dick Pearson, Bob Henry, ? Marriot, Leon Rauch, ? Bowen, and Bill Davis. (Courtesy R. Kelley.)

Barry Enoch, ST-1 Alfa platoon, maintains vigilance of the perimeter as the army Huey helicopter flies away after inserting the SEAL squad. (Courtesy C. Maury.)

Lt. Rip Bliss, ST-1 Alfa platoon, walks out of the burning hooch with a bag full of Vietcong documents as Mike Beenam stands guard with his M60 machine gun. This mission was to destroy a Vietcong village on December 19, 1968, and relocate civilians to a safe area. (Courtesy C. Maury.)

Steve Frisk, ST-1 Alfa platoon, fires a law rocket at a nearby hooch, which went up in flames, as Mike Beenam stands guard with his M60 machine gun. (Courtesy C. Maury.)

"Raid Frees 19 Vietnamese POWs" is the newspaper headline about a Navy SEAL dawn raid on a Vietcong prison camp in the Mekong Delta, An Xuyen Province, Vietnam, on November 22, 1970. SEALs engaged in a firefight; 18 enemies fled the camp, and 19 POWs were discovered as well as weapons and supplies. At left, ST-1 Whiskey platoon chief Pat McKnight keeps a close watch over a section of the POW camp. Below, Chuck Miller, Zulu platoon radioman, radio handset in hand, looks out from one of the camp hooches with cups stacked up on a table. (Both, courtesy D. Peterson.)

An ST-1 squad poses with a small portion of the weapons and ammunition cache they discovered at a Vietcong base camp in the Rung Sat Zone. The SEAL squad was inserted by helicopter at dawn and to their surprise landed into the middle of a Vietcong base camp. The platoon point man initiated with a silenced submachine gun, using the element of surprise on a sleeping enemy, resulting in this six-man SEAL squad taking over the base camp. From left to right are ? Totten; Doc Weaver; Lieutenant, Junior Grade, Schwartely; Walt Gustavel; and Robert Kelley. (Courtesy R. Kelley.)

Intelligence from a previous operation provided information on the location of a Vietcong cache of B-40 rockets. From left to right, Vietnamese SEAL Gieng Nguyen and Victor platoon members Terry Bryant, leading petty officer; Barry Schreckengost, radioman; Michael Wood, point man; and Lt. Roger Clapp, OIC, stand over the captured B-40 rockets.

Shawn Tran, at right holding a microphone, was a Vietnamese interpreter for several ST-1 platoons in Vietnam. Here Shawn is preparing a psychological operations helicopter speaker system for a PSYOP supporting intelligence operations to entice known Vietcong to Cheiu Hoi or surrender. Shawn is also a local Escondido resident and tax consultant to several SEALs today. The person behind the speakers is unidentified.

This Zulu platoon Christmas postcard photograph was taken against the platoon hooch and bunker at Solid Anchor. The card was sent to platoon family and friends to let them know they were all okay. From left to right are (first row) Wendell Hedge, unidentified VN interpreter, Moses Marquez, Jack Shultz, and unidentified VN interpreter; (second row) Don Futrell, Dan Peterson, Tom Harris, and Tom Richards; (third row) Gary Lawrence, Marcus Arroyo, Chuck Miller, and Dave Roland. (Courtesy D. Peterson.)

Bill Doyle, Victor platoon leading petty officer, examines the canopy damage of the X-ray platoon medium SEAL support craft (MSSC) caused by a Vietcong B-40 rocket. At right, Lt. Mike Collins, X-ray platoon commander, paid the ultimate price and lost his life from the damage caused by the Vietcong rocket attack on the platoon MSSC.

ST-3 platoon personnel from an NSW Task Unit assaulted this oil rig during early operations of Desert Storm. The SEAL squad is near the bridge ramp with Iraqi prisoners lying down on the deck.

An NSW Task Unit Sierra rigid inflatable boat (RIB), floating in the water with SEALs and explosive ordnance disposal (EOD) personnel, moves up close to an Iraqi contact mine floating on the surface in the Northern Arabian Gulf (NAG) during the early morning hours as it drifts close by to the anchored Kuwait ship *Sawahil*, nicknamed "Happy Duck." This ship is fully loaded with 105-mm artillery ammo and Exocet missiles. (Author's collection.)

ST-3 Golf platoon conducts an underwater hydrographic survey of Kuwait harbor while on a USS *Tarwana* Amphibious Readiness Group (ARG) deployment to Kuwait that coincided with the one-year anniversary of Kuwait liberation. The combat swimmer pair is diving with a Draeger LAR-V oxygen rebreather and using the Swimmer Area Navigation system to record swimmer lanes and depth soundings, formerly done by Frogmen surface swimmers with lead lines and slates. (Author's collection.)

ST-3 Golf platoon demonstrates close-quarter battle tactics and techniques to the Kuwaiti Emeri Guard at the police kill house near downtown Kuwait City as part of the ARG foreign internal defense (FID) exercise. FID training also included explosive entry techniques, AT4 rocket firing, rappelling, and fast-roping. (Author's collection.)

A fire team of SEALs transition
from underwater in San Diego
Bay over the beach wearing
Draeger LAR-V oxygen
rebreathers and carrying
MP-5 9-mm submachine
guns. (Author's collection.)

A SEAL squad fast-ropes from a
MH-53J Pave Low III helicopter
and inserts on the bridge of
a vehicle cargo ship during
a ship-boarding exercise.

A SEAL sniper team transitions from underwater in the San Diego Bay over the beach and sets up an initial observation point wearing Ghillie suits and carrying 300 WINMAG sniper rifles and carbine automatic M4A1 5.56-mm rifles. (Author's collection.)

A SEAL combat swimmer pair keeps their water skills up to date by conducting underwater navigation training, diving with Draeger LAR-V oxygen rebreathers and using a compass board. (Author's collection.)

These photographs represent the sea and air operations of the sea, air, and land (SEAL) name. At left, a SEAL supervises a Kuwaiti Emeri Guard officer conducting fast-rope training during an FID exercise. Below, a SEAL squad looks down to the Imperial Beach area below while connected to a Maguire Rig attached to a navy CH-46 helicopter as they fly over the outlying landing field (OLF) Imperial Beach. (Author's collection.)

A pair of SEAL combat swimmers begins to transition from underwater, observing their beach exit point before crossing the beach. These SEALs are wearing face mesh for camouflage and are carrying M4A1 5.56-mm carbine rifles. (Author's collection.)

A SEAL combat swimmer, wearing a U.S. Divers oxygen rebreather called the FROG, begins surfacing while maintaining course with the swimmer attack board. (Author's collection.)

Special Operations Chief Chris Beck, patrolling as a rear security on a ST-5 search mission in Baghdad, combs through prison cells and underground tunnels for the American pilot and POW/MIA Scott Speicher. Chris located Speicher's initials on a prison cell wall. Below, a SEAL desert patrol vehicle (DPV) prepares for a mission in Afghanistan. The DPV was built by Chenoweth Racing Products, Inc., in El Cajon, California.

This group of SEALs is from the Naval Special Operations Force (NAVSOF) detachment and part of the larger Special Operations Force unit at Kandahar, Iraq.

Master Chief Bryan Yarbro (left) and Chief Derek ("Pepper") Williams inspect a building, in rubble, while conducting an area recon on a Kawasaki Teryx quad and performing engagement operations in the southern Al Jazeera Desert of southwest Iraq. (Courtesy B. Yarbro.)

ST-1 Victor platoon is pictured outside their barracks at Dong Tam, Vietnam, in May 1971. From left to right are (first row) Mike Walsh, Don Barnes, Bruce Russell, Frank Richard, John Cymbal, and unidentified VN interpreter; (second row) Michael Wood, Woody Shoemaker, Roger Clapp, Jim Young, Barry Schreckengost, Tipton Amen, and Terry Bryant. Marshal Daugherty, another SEAL platoon member, is not pictured. (Author's collection.)

The author, covered in mud and holding a 5.56-mm Stoner submachine gun, sits in the Victor platoon MSSC next to Gieng Nguyen, a Vietnamese SEAL, while they are transiting back from a mission. (Author's collection.)

# Three

# SEAL DELIVERY VEHICLE TEAM

During World War II, the Italians and the British pioneered the use of small submersibles for stealthy attacks on shipping. During the five-year period following the end of World War II, little work was done on swimmer delivery vehicles. Because of the war in Korea, in 1952, there was increased interest in the development of SEAL delivery vehicles (SDV) or Swimmer Propulsion Units (SPU), as they were called then. A number of wet and dry vehicles were constructed between 1952 and 1955.

This chapter covers the SDVs, which originally were part of the UDT and SEAL teams before they became their own command. On the West Coast, ST-1, UDT-11, and UDT-12 each had an SDV platoon as part of their command. During this early period, many wet submersibles were experimented with and tested, eventually narrowing the candidate SDVs down to a couple of companies. Some pictures will show the early SDVs and the SDV platoons while assigned to one of those commands.

On May 1, 1983, UDT-12 was renamed and became SDVT-1, home based on NAB Coronado but transferring physical location from the ocean side of the Silver Strand to the bay side by Pier 13. SDV command was made of SDV platoons, but during this period, a Dry Deck Shelter (DDS) platoon was added to the command upon the arrival of the new deep submergence system that holds SDVs and attaches to the hull of selected submarines. This new DDS capability, combined with the SDV capability, brought forward an era of innovative development in underwater operations. In 1996, SDVT-1 moved from Coronado, California, to Ford Island in Pearl Harbor, where it is now stationed in Pearl City, Hawaii.

The French Loral PR-77 was tested in 1964, and a team of representatives from Navy Mine Defense Laboratory, Panama City, Florida, visited France to investigate this vehicle. It was purchased and tested. It was designed for two scuba-equipped divers side by side with a large Plexiglas windows for outside visibility.

At least 30 combat swimmer delivery vehicles were proposed or built in the United States since 1952, and up to 52 vehicles were considered for underwater swimmers. Below, technicians are adjusting the motor on the submersible canoe being tested at the NAB Coronado pool.

Photographer's Mate Lou Boyles, UDT-11, is dressed in a full wet suit, fins, and mask ready to dive in the Seahorse submersible, a two-man, wet swimmer delivery vehicle. The Seahorse is on a shop dolly in the UDT-11 compound.

A General Dynamics/Convair model 14, later a MK-6, swimmer delivery vehicle was a four-man wet submersible vehicle capable of a sustained 5-knot cruising speed for eight hours. The pilot sits in the forward compartment piloting the SDV using the top-mounted obstacle avoidance sonar.

UDT-11 SDV platoon members prepare to launch the Seahorse submersible on a training mission in Subic Bay in 1964. From left to right are ? Arsenaldt; Roger Cook, pilot; and Bob Clark, navigator. (Courtesy R. Cook.)

From left to right, Bob Clark and David Devine prepare the Seahorse for a dive outside the SDV facility on the military base in Subic Bay in 1964. The people in back are unidentified. (Courtesy R. Cook.)

Lt. Tom Moser, officer in charge of ST-1 Delta platoon, rides in the forward compartment of the SDV ready to conduct a MK-6 SDV training dive in Subic Bay, Philippines. The SDV was piloted by a UDT Frogman, but SEALs conducted familiarization training in the SDV to ensure they were familiar with SDV operational and emergency procedures. The person in back is unidentified. (Courtesy D. Peterson.)

Before the current Dry Deck Shelter, submarines, and MK-8 SDVs, there was the LPSS *Grayback* submarine with its converted surface missile launching bays turned into MK-6 and MK-7 SDV hangar bays. Above is a view looking out of the *Grayback* hangar bay to a ST-1 MK-6 SDV rolled out on deck with submarine crew on watch while pier side in Subic Bay in 1970. (Courtesy R. Kelly.)

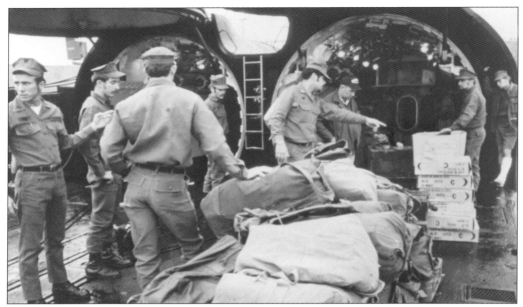

SEALs load the hangars of the USS *Grayback*, LPSS 574. In 1972, U.S. Pacific Command was authorized to execute Operation Thunderhead, where SEALs were employed from SDVs to assist in the rescue of American POWs planning to escape Vietnam via the Red River to the Gulf of Tonkin. Mission planning, training, and rehearsal were conducted, but the mission was aborted during initial execution. This was the first combat use of SDVs. (Courtesy T. Reeves.)

USS *Grayback* crewmen and UDT Frogmen roll the MK-7 SDV across the deck into one of the two *Grayback* hangars. For UDT-11 SDV platoon, Tom Edwards was the SDV navigator, and Lieutenant Lutz was the SDV pilot supporting the ST-1 Alfa platoon POW recovery mission.

Lt. Spence Dry conducts a mission briefing with members of ST-1 Alfa platoon on deck and in front of the USS *Grayback* hangars. Lieutenant Dry was killed and two others injured during a helicopter drop attempting to rendezvous with the *Grayback*. Moki Martin rallied the survivors until rescue eight hours later. From left to right, the faces visible are Moki Martin, Rick Hetzell, Spence Dry, Bob Hooke, and Scott Shaw of UDT-11. (Courtesy T. Reeves.)

Alfa platoon squad paddles an IBS back to the USS *Grayback* while conducting dry deck launch and recovery training in preparation for Operation Thunderhead. USS *Grayback* is surfaced with the hangar door open. (Courtesy T. Reeves.)

This SDVT-1 Command photograph was taken in 1983 when it moved to the bay side of NAB Coronado. SDVT-1 added a new type of SEAL platoon, called Dry Deck Shelter (DDS) platoon. DDS is a deep submergence system that holds SDVs and attaches to the hull of selected submarines. Lt. Cdr. Eric Olson (first row, fourth from left) later became the first SEAL four-star admiral and commander of Special Operations Command. In the first row at far right is Ens. Brian Losey, who later became a rear admiral. (Author's collection.)

DDS platoon SEALs wrestle with an SDV during launch and recovery operations aboard an underway submarine. This view is from inside the DDS hangar looking out the 9-foot opening to the DDS track and cradle system, where the deck crewmen recover the SDV onto the cradle. (Author's collection.)

A DDS deck crewman swims a waterproofed outboard motor to the surface, where SEALs hang on to their combat rubber raiding craft (CRRC) floating above and tied to the submarine below during mass swimmer lock-out operations. (Author's collection.)

A MK-8 Mod-0 SDV conducts a final approach to rendezvous with the USS *Kamehameha* carrying a dual DDS. The SDV homes in on a beacon in the buoy floating above the submarine with the DDS track and cradle out and ready to receive the SDV. (Author's collection.)

Submarine availability can be sparse to maintain qualifications for SDV, DDS personnel, and submarine launch and recovery operations, so the Subtrap was developed to simulate submarine underway operations. Subtrap is a large deck with ballast controls for underwater depth control while being towed by a surface vessel. Above, the Subtrap crew stands by for SDV recovery. Below, the Subtrap pilot and copilot use the ballast controls to maintain the proper depth during Subtrap operations off of San Diego. (Both, author's collection.)

The SDV pilot and navigator swim a 100-pound MK-5 limpet assembly module (LAM) from the aft compartment of the SDV bottomed up under a target ship during a live-demolition ship SINKEX. The pilot and navigator inflate the LAM air bladders to hold the demolition in place, insert the safe and arming device into the end cap of the LAM, and initiate the timer device. (Both, author's collection.)

MK-8 Mod-0 SDV is tied off to a Long Beach oil rig diagonal support leg. The SDV pilot and navigator swim a mock detonation cord trunk line around three of the four oil rig legs, connecting three 100-pound MK-6 practice LAMs in training for operations against maritime facilities prior to the Desert Storm war in the Persian Gulf. (Author's collection.)

SDV operator emplaces a 100-pound MK-6 PLAM practice demolition to one of the oil rig legs and then connects it to the practice detonation cord connected to two other demolitions. The demolition is emplaced at 70 feet underwater. (Author's collection.)

During Operation Desert Storm (1990–1991), the Kuwaiti Coast Guard ship *Sawahil*, nicknamed "Happy Duck," was converted by the NSW Task Group and Kuwait Navy (KUN) for helicopter and SDV operations. A KUN crane operator lifts the SDV Task Element MK-8 Mod-0 SDV for the SDV platoon's mine search operations in the NAG. This was the second use by the United States of combat submersibles, with the first in Haiphong Harbor, Vietnam. (Author's collection.)

SDV, with the SEAL remote imaging periscope (SRIP), conducts a training surface reconnaissance mission against the KUN ship *Al Sanbouk*, a missile boat in the NAG, in preparation for hydrographic reconnaissance mission of planned beach landing sites. (Author's collection.)

In this group photograph are members of the NSW Task Unit Sierra, NSW Task Element Kilo, SDV platoon, KUN ship crew, and KUN commodore staff on the flight deck of the KUN ship *Sawahil* immediately following the liberation of Kuwait. The *Sawahil* was originally designed to house

SDV platoon tow sled crewmen hand-signal to the tow sled master aboard the KUN ship *Instiglal*, indicating the SDV is secure and ready to transit to the SDV mine search mission location in the NAG. Ironically, after many years of SDVs training from the Dry Deck Shelter (DDS) and submarines, the second wartime use of combat submersibles is conducted towed from a foreign surface ship. This illustrates NSW capability to adapt and overcome a situation, since the NAG waters were too shallow for submarine operations.

35 oil field workers but during Desert Storm accommodated over 75 U.S. and Kuwaiti personnel conducting Special Operation Forces (SOF) operations in the NAG. (Author's collection.)

Lt. Cdr. Michael Wood, SDV Task Element commander, and two KUN ship *Sawahil* sailors raise the Kuwait flag on top the Kubbar Island lighthouse after the Iraqis had deserted the island. KUN fleet—*Al Sanbouk, Instiglal,* and *Sawahil*—personnel were ecstatic at this symbolic gesture of returning Kubbar Island back to Kuwait. (Author's collection.)

The pilot and navigator of the newer MK-8 Mod-1 SDV look back and communicate over the newer SDV antennae system to the dive supervisor ashore for permission to commence the training dive in Glorietta Bay at NAB Coronado. This generation SDV can carry six SEALs and transit at faster speeds for longer periods of time. (Author's collection.)

An SH-60 helicopter lowers a SEAL for personnel transfer to the surfaced DDS, carried by an older former ballistic missile submarine. Newer boomer Trident submarines have been converted for SOF and cruise missile missions and will be the clandestine platform of choice for the near future. (Author's collection.)

A four-man fire team of SEALs inserted ashore from an SDV conducts nighttime emplacement of unattended ground sensors in support of a test of the sensor network. Future global war on terror missions will require SDVs and SEALs to be more involved in sensor placements than direct action missions. (Author's collection.)

The SDV pilot and navigator remove this sensor gateway buoy from the back of the SDV, assembling the buoy underwater and preparing it for unattended operations. This is a training dive for the operators to learn the tactics and procedures of the gateway buoy emplacement. SDVs will be used to clandestinely insert SEALs for both underwater and land sensor emplacements. (Author's collection.)

SDVT-1 Bravo platoon, also known as "Dirty Stinking Dogs," is pictured with the Coronado Bay Bridge in the background. From left to right are (first row) Tim Hillock, Abe Laird, John Hall, Brian Yarbro, and Guiermo Silva; (second row) Jim Morel, Dale Griffith, Marcus Presson, William Palombi, W. D. Green, Joe Herman, Bruce Soltis, Roberto Duff, and Michael Wood. (Author's collection.)

The author, Michael P. Wood, is standing guard at a beach berm after crossing the beach at night from the SDV left underwater in the San Diego Bay as other SDV tacticians come ashore. Wood is wearing a wet suit, camouflage top, and Draeger LAR-V oxygen rebreather while carrying an H&K MP5 navy–model weapon with suppressor and a Dukane pinger receiver hanging from his vest. (Author's collection.)

*Four*

# BASIC UNDERWATER DEMOLITION/ SEAL TRAINING

The essence of BUD/S training has remained the same from the earliest days at Fort Pierce, Florida, to today in Coronado, California: to transform healthy but unsure "tadpoles" into self-assured, fully web-footed Frogmen capable of attaining feats others would deem unattainable. The training phases have remained the same at three phases, including basic conditioning phase, diving phase, and land warfare phase. The phase order has switched occasionally, but the training content has remained constant. Another constant has been the concept of Hell Week, which sets BUD/S apart from any other U.S. military or even international military training program. Even during the short period Hell Week was suspended, the training compensated in other ways to make sure tadpoles received the full benefit. Psychologists, educators, and military planners have all conducted exhaustive studies on the "type" of person who successfully completes BUD/S training, studying body type, background, sports experience, education, and medical history. Theories were developed, and changes in the training program affected all with the hope of reducing the standard 70 percent attrition rate to an achievable 50 percent so the total number of SEALs can be increased. Generally the results are to no avail, with some minor fluctuations in attrition. An epiphany occurred that the 70 percent attrition would not change much, but the numbers of SEALs could be increased by better screening and quality of trainees entering BUD/S; as well, with vigilant medical attention during training and recouping, injured trainees have improved the number of SEALs going out the door.

BUD/S training organization has changed significantly through the years, from Fort Pierce and Hawaii with organized training during World War II, to UDT in-house training during and after the Korean War and back to organized training with a training unit on each coast in Little Creek, Virginia, and Coronado, California. Training was later consolidated on the West Coast at NAB Coronado, initially under the auspices of the Naval Amphibious School and later under the command of NSWC. BUD/S is now a command of its own under the Naval Special Warfare Center (NAVSPECWARCEN) major command, all still located on NAB Coronado.

Class 46 responds to the classic instructor words of the time to "hit the bay" during the first phase of training. Reasons for the class's transgression are known only to the instructor standing on the quay wall. Even the slightly warmer waters of San Diego Bay can seem to be freezing after an hour of standing still and singing songs.

This class "hits the ocean," where the water is significantly colder. The students line up arm in arm and march into the surf zone to learn if they stay connected as a team, they can stay upright in the surf. If one member lets go, it affects the whole line. They also learn to encourage each other to stick it out when the cold water starts taking its effect.

First-phase BUD/S students feel the pain of log physical training (PT) no matter what year it occurs. Although the pain is the same, the time frame is different between these early-1960s and mid-1970s pictures of log PT on the Silver Strand in Coronado, California. Above, the log team work breaks down and one member pays the price. At right, the team is in unison, and though all experience the struggle, they learn that teamwork, and not brute strength alone, helps accomplish the task.

Early-1960s first-phase Hell Week students appear to be having a fun time playing "king of the mountain" on their IBS, floating in a muddy pond as a nearby instructor closely monitors to make sure the tadpoles play fair.

The facial expressions prove that the first-phase students really enjoy their muddy experience.

First-phase Hell Week mud flats can test the strongest of men as the body must overcome the constant resistance of the sticky, slimy mud. It is difficult to tell if these are humans or some type of muddy centipede. These are actually teams of students conducting line races in the mud. It pays to be a winner.

A Hell Week student takes time to enjoy his mud-covered sandwich while sitting in the middle of a mud puddle fully encrusted in the sweet-smelling mud of the Southbay tidal area next to the Silver Strand. People pay big money for this kind of mud-bath treatment.

Students bury their heads in the sand as the half-pound blocks of TNT detonate alongside them on the sand berm to test them for their ability to remain calm when all is going to hell around them.

First-phase instructor Dick Allen exposes students to sand appreciation as they sit in a huddle learning how to keep going no matter how sandy and gritty they might become.

The BUD/S PT instructor on the platform holds his fist in the air, indicating for the students to be quiet and listen for the next exercise command. Many tadpoles through time have exercised on this grinder at the NAVSPECWARCEN in Coronado, California. (Author's collection.)

A trainee begins to show the strain of hours-long PT evolution as he yells out "Hooyahs" during the exercise. (Author's collection.)

The first-phase boat crew conducts surf passage and attempts to paddle in unison as the 4-foot hollow wave crashes just behind with the potential to overturn their boat. The bowman on the left digs in with his paddle as the bowman on the right looks back at the wave. (Author's collection.)

The class proctor and instructor instruct the officers, who are the boat crew captains, on their surf passage evolution while some of the boat crews stand at attention next to their IBS with the Coronado high-rises in the background. (Author's collection.)

The starboard bowman digs in with his paddle as the bow of his IBS hits the white water from an incoming wave and momentarily knocks him off balance during surf passage training on the Silver Strand in Coronado. (Author's collection.)

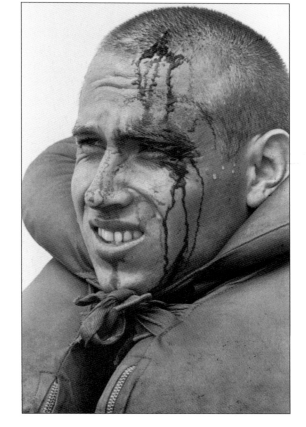

A student is injured from a paddle hitting him in the head. He was not interested in his injury and just wanted to return to his boat crew out in the surf. Medical attention was immediately provided to the student, and the injury was very minor despite what the photograph shows. (Author's collection.)

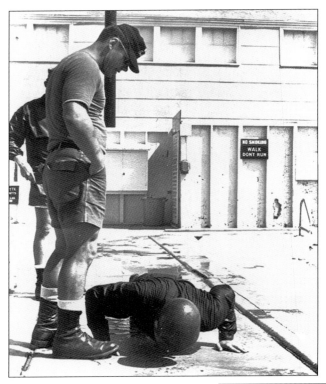

BUD/S or UDTRA (Underwater Demolition Training) instructors leave a long-lasting and sometimes lifelong impression with their students, especially first-phase instructors. At left is Instructor Chief Terry "Mother" Moy providing a student one-on-one instruction on pushups. Following a leave to Rhode Island, Chief Moy returned to training with a brass bell for students to ring out and signal they want to quit. Below are Instructor Weaver (left) and Senior Chief Dick Allen (right). Each class has one instructor in each phase who serves as the class proctor for that phase. First-phase proctors are remembered for life.

A student uses the above-the-line technique for quickly crossing the slide for life obstacle at the obstacle course on the Silver Strand next to the BUD/S training area and other SEAL team areas. Another student climbs up the pole to start his crossing of the slide for life. (Author's collection.)

A student uses his legs and hands to climb to the top of the cargo net obstacle and must cross over the top and climb back down as quickly as possible to complete the obstacle course in time. Another student is not far behind at the bottom. (Author's collection.)

First-phase tadpoles line up around the NAB Coronado pool and watch as the instructor's hands are tied behind his back and his ankles tied together to demonstrate drown proofing. Drown proofing is important because it demonstrates to students that if wounded or injured they can still swim. Many SEALs in combat have swum to safety while seriously wounded and in some cases carrying another injured SEAL. (Author's collection.)

The student's hands and feet are tied, and he swims to the bottom of the pool, picking up a face mask in his mouth and swimming back up to the surface. He demonstrates calm and the ability to swim while tied up, proving the drown-proofing technique. (Author's collection.)

Students stand against the NAB Coronado pool wall shivering while waiting to go back into the pool following their drown-proofing training. Instructor Rick Knepper, with clipboard, does not appear too concerned with their shivering symptoms. (Author's collection.)

A Hell Week student showing the strain and pain of three days of no sleep and constant activity decides that he has had enough and rings the bell, indicating he wants to quit BUD/S. Before Chief Moy introduced the bell, students would knock on the instructor's door or had to stand in front of a Chiquita banana full-length poster waiting for the instructor's attention: "What do you want, banana?" (Author's collection.)

A second-phase diving student wearing open-circuit twin scuba bottles with a double hose regulator responds to a command to commence the dive.

This second-phase diving instructor briefs the students on the open-circuit dive they will be commencing in San Diego Bay. The briefing is being held in the BUD/S dive locker. (Author's collection.)

A second-phase diving instructor, Jim Day, sets up a MK-15 constant partial-pressure oxygen rebreather for an upcoming student dive in the San Diego Bay. (Author's collection.)

A second-phase diving instructor appears upside down free diving from the surface, checking on a student learning how to ditch and don his twin open-circuit scuba tanks during an open-circuit familiarization dive in the BUD/S combat training tank at NAB Coronado.

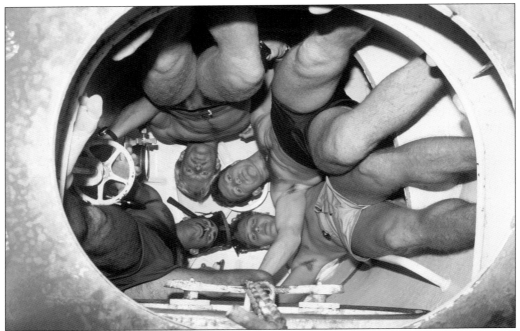

Above, second-phase students and instructors load into the diving tower submarine escape trunk to conduct submarine lock-in and lock-out training from the tower escape trunk. Once the trunk hatch is closed, it is flooded with water, then pressurized and equalized with the water pressure in the 50-foot dive tower. Escape trunk quarters are very tight. Below, the pressure is equalized, the escape hatch is opened, and the instructor prepares to set up the ascent line to the surface. (Author's collection.)

Two second-phase dive tower instructors help a student transfer from the roving dive bell to the 50-foot dive bell in preparation for conducting buoyant ascent training in the 50-foot dive tower near the ocean on the Silver Strand. Buoyant ascent training is conducted to simulate escaping from a submarine in shallow water. (Author's collection.)

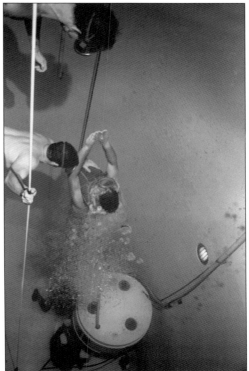

Head back, hands overhead, continuous exhalation, and life jacket fully inflated, the student speeds to the surface. A dive tower instructor positioned at a 25-foot depth ensures the student conducts a controlled ascent to the surface 50 feet above. (Author's collection.)

This third-phase land warfare student uses all his strength to hold onto the obstacle horn and resist the wave action while loading the 40-pound haversack of explosives onto the obstacle at San Clemente Island (SCI) BUD/S camp. (Author's collection.)

This class of third-phase students prepares both the 40-pound haversacks of explosives and the large reel of detonation cord for the trunk line as they prepare to set explosives on the field of underwater obstacles at BUD/S beach at SCI.

A third-phase student free dives 15 feet underwater and ties a 40-pound haversack of explosives onto the horns of an obstacle in the surf zone off BUD/S beach at SCI. BUD/S students completed attaching explosive to the whole field of obstacles above and below the water. They then attached a detonation cord trunk line connecting all of the explosives. Detonation sent a plume of water 100 feet high. (Author's collection.)

These third-phase students prepare a different type of explosives, MK-8 hose, and begin to weave the lengths of explosive hose into a matte formation, a technique used for clearing boat lanes in reefs at amphibious landing sites.

Third-phase students learn how to assemble and disassemble an M-16 rifle during their weapons classroom lesson at BUD/S. Below, Instructor Bill Cheatham Reed inspects a student's weapon and shows him the carbon on his bolt assembly.

A second-phase dive pair exits the water on the Silver Strand and crosses the beach wearing the Draeger LAR-V UBA and carrying an M-16 rifle.

Third-phase BUD/S students are pictured here firing Beretta 9-mm pistols at the North Island Naval Air Station pistol range.

Class 55, a winter class from 1968, form up for a graduation picture outside the BUD/S administrative office on the bay side of NAB Coronado. Class 55 started with 130 trainees and graduated with 34, resulting in a 74-percent attrition rate. Many members of this class remain residents of San Diego County to this day. (Author's collection.)

These four officers—from left to right, Lt. Cdr. Don Ridgeway, Lt. Karl Heinz, Lt. (jg) Marshall Daugherty, and Ens. Michael Wood—were all prior enlisted men in the Class 55 graduation photograph and later reunited following commissioning for this photograph in front of the current BUD/S building on the ocean side of the NAB Coronado. (Author's collection.)

# Five

# SEALs and Sea Lions

This chapter covers the beginning when U.S. Navy SEALs worked closely with California sea lions (*Zalophus californianus*) in Project Quick Find, part of the navy's early marine mammal program. During this period, SEALs of San Diego left the jungles of Vietnam to train sea lions to mark and aid in recovery of inert ASROCs from the war reserve stockpiles to ensure the inert weapons were ready for service. The sea lions were capable of diving as deep as 750 feet to locate and mark these weapons on the ocean bottom. Project Quick Find, initially located in Hawaii, moved to Point Loma and NAB Coronado, where SEALs initially joined forces with EOD personnel. Later a Navy Special Warfare command, IUWG-1, took command of the program.

Navy SEALs trained the sea lions to listen for and identify special frequency pingers attached to the missiles in the deep cold water but then to use their underwater vision to locate and mark the missiles with a special grabber device attached to a recovery line. Project Quick Find SEALs and sea lions conducted numerous ASROC recovery missions in California, Virginia, and Florida. Navy SEALs along with marine mammal experts and veterinarians also conducted sea lion captures at San Nicholas Island under the close guidance of the California Marine Mammal Protection Act to recruit yearling sea lions into the project. SEALs and sea lions were teamed up into trainer and animal pairs to work together through the initial training phases of the complex, deep water recovery missions. Throughout the process, the sea lions were more than free to swim away but always returned and completed their tasks. The SEALs all completed animal behavioral psychology courses to prepare for their mission to work with mature sea lions, such as Fatman, Aikahi, and Snitch, and younger sea lions, such as Point Loma–recruit Sinbad and San Nicholas–born Papillon.

This chapter only covers Project Quick Find, but this was merely one portion of the navy's more extensive marine mammal program, which also included the porpoises in Project Short Time that conducted anti-swimmer protection. Later this NSW effort was transferred back to the navy and included SEALs, marines, and EOD personnel of the Very Shallow Water Mine Countermeasures (VSW-MCM) program.

A California sea lion (*Zalophus californianus*) named Fatman dives 90 feet underwater to attach a grabber device to the tail cone of a mock-up ASROC missile 2 miles off the coast of Point Loma. This training grabber device does not lock onto the tail cone coated with black grease. When the grabber is recovered to the surface, the grease indicates the sea lion hit the right location. (Author's collection.)

Sea lion trainer Dan Peterson prepares to walk his sea lion, Buckwheat, from the floating pen to the boat for training out at sea. The trainer whistle is used as a bridge for positive reinforcement of rewards of smelt and mackerel. The sea lion is wearing a harness with a leash attachment worn only when training. Buckwheat was the first naïve sea lion to be trained from basic to advanced behaviors by a navy SEAL. (Author's collection.)

This Quick Find 36-foot work barge, towing a Z-bird inflatable, transits to the training dive area 4 miles off the coast of Point Loma, where water depth ranges from 250 to 500 feet. On board is the ASROC missile mock-up, a davit, and a winch for raising and lowering the training target. The Quick Find trainers make the 20-mile round-trip transit from NAB Coronado to the training area five days a week regardless of weather conditions. (Author's collection.)

Trainer Bud Dennehy places a D-9 grabber onto the nose of Aikahi the sea lion during a training dive off the coast of Point Loma, California. (Author's collection.)

An ASROC missile is fired from a navy ship during a quality assurance test (QUAST) off of SCI. Soon after the missile firing, the Project Quick Find sea lions located and marked it for recovery as well as the trajectory data. (Courtesy U.S. Navy.)

Sea lions initially localize the missile by a 9-khz pinger audible to them and then use their low light visibility to place the grabber device onto the missile tail cone for recovery by a surface vessel winch. Below, Quick Find SEALs reach over the aft stern of the landing craft utility (LCU) to guide the real ASROC missile onto the aft deck of the LCU. (Both, author's collection.)

Trainer Tom Waples gives the sea lion the hand signal to enter the water. The sea lion enters the cold water off the coast of Point Loma, California. The tether line connected to the sea lion's harness indicates the animal is conducting basic training and not yet trusted to return to the inflatable boat of its own free will. Once an animal displays confidence to return, the tether line is removed. (Author's collection.)

From left to right are the Quick Find officer in command, Lt. Marshall Daugherty; unidentified; Harry Nush; and Bud Dennehy, holding one of the sea lions and the grabber devices with the mock-up ASROC to the side at SCI. Lieutenant Daugherty took their training to SCI to increase their access to deeper water and focus on deepwater ASROC recoveries in up to 750 feet of sea water. (Author's collection.)

Trainer Dave Dennehy places a probe-shaped marker on a bite plate that the sea lion bites and swims down 40 feet to a mock mine shape (a device that looks like an underwater explosive) at SCI. This was the beginning of Project Quick Find shifting from marking and recovering ASROC missiles to marking and recovering underwater mines. (Author's collection.)

A trainer removes the body harness device from the sea lion at the end of the training day as the sun sets at NAB Coronado, California. (Author's collection.)

This group of California sea lions (*Zalophus californianus*) is alerted to an intrusion and begins waking up and moving to the surf zone at San Nicholas Island rookery. Below, a group of veterinarians, doctors, and navy SEALs huddle to discuss their capture approach path to the rookery of sea lions. The group goal was to capture two-year-old males for potential training in the marine mammal program. The capture was fully monitored and conducted in accordance with the Marine Mammal Act and the California state capture permit. (Both, author's collection.)

Some navy SEAL captors decide to approach the herd from the surf zone so they are running into the herd as the group runs to the safety of the surf zone. Below, navy SEALs Rick Hetzell (left) and Dan Peterson (right) use their hoop nets to hold three sea lions until the veterinarian can inspect the animals for health and sex status. (Both, author's collection.)

Navy SEAL Dan Peterson tries to calm a young sea lion just captured in a hoop net at a rookery on San Nicholas Island. A dozen sea lions were initially captured and given complete physicals and blood work, and some were released back to the rookery. (Author's collection.)

A group of veterinarians and SEALs hold the hind flippers of young California sea lions waiting to have their sex checked at a rookery on San Nicholas Island. Young males were the desired sex to capture for the marine mammal program. From left to right are Lt. Don Ridgeway, veterinarian Bob Gunnels, Dan Peterson, unidentified, Marine Fisheries observer, Jack Kennedy, and Rob Horseman. (Author's collection.)

This group of captors gathers around and helps cool down the recently captured young male sea lions by placing their cages at the beginning of the surf zone to ensure their body temperature remains at safe limits. (Author's collection.)

A young male sea lion rests up against his cage and looks out at the nearby pool of ocean water. (Author's collection.)

This small group of navy SEALs and EOD personnel are Project Quick Find "plank owners," which indicates they were original members of the team when the program was officially accepted by the U.S. Navy. From left to right are Tom McHugh, Gordon Sybrant, Michael Wood, Rick Hetzel, Dan Peterson, and Lt. Paul Plumb. This photograph was taken during a QUAST recovery in Florida. (Author's collection.)

Author Michael Wood sits against the SCI fish house wall as the young sea lion seeks refuge from the cold floor and rests on the warm body heat of the author's legs. This young sea lion later was named "Papillon" for his multiple attempts to escape. Papillon was a very smart animal that learned all the marine mammal basic behaviors in a short period of time. (Author's collection.)

# *Six*

# COMMUNITY RELATIONS

SEALs and Frogs have been part of the San Diego community since World War II. Their role in the community has varied throughout the years but covers a broad range of interaction and involvement, from direct involvement and leadership to just being a good neighbor. Many have been very involved in their communities both as active duty military and as residents.

As military representatives, SEALs and Frogs have participated in many parades, fairs, other special events, and football games, providing military displays, operational demonstrations, and speeches. The biggest of these events was a very extensive and elaborate NSW Fourth of July demonstration in Coronado, California, following the half marathon and parade. NSW parachuters have skydived from above and parachuted over the Hotel Del Coronado and Chart House and landed on the Coronado golf course or into Glorietta Bay. SEALs, Frogs, and Combatant Craft operators have driven high-speed boats, detonated explosives, jumped out of helicopters, and operated SDV Sharks all to support the annual Coronado Fourth of July celebrations. People from all over the country would come to Coronado to watch this UDT/SEAL demonstration. Frogs and SEALs have used their operational skills also to directly support the surrounding communities, in some cases by using explosives to clear ship wreckage from a beach or damaged pier pilings from the water, all to help the community clear hazardous conditions.

As residents, many UDT/SEALs play an active role in their community, having served as mayors of towns, city representatives, volunteers at libraries and hospitals, and later serving second careers as doctors, policemen, and firemen. Some, such as Moki Martin, a resident of Coronado, started and hosts the annual Super Frog triathlon competition in Coronado and Imperial Beach every year, which draws triathletes from all over the country just to be in a Super Frog. Many retired and active duty Frogs and SEALs end up homesteading in the San Diego area and calling it home.

UDT Frogmen ride a float during a downtown San Diego Columbus Day parade in October 1975. These Frogmen exhibit paddling an IBS and space capsule recovery while wearing the traditional UDT trunks and life jackets. Below, from left to right, two unidentified, Don Glasser, and John Wanker from UDT teams pose paddling the IBS while wearing face masks on their head.

One SEAL parachutist appears to be floating over the Hotel Del Coronado as he guides his T-10 parachute toward Glorietta Bay to land in the water. Below, the Leap Frogs navy parachute team free falls from a 12,000-foot altitude and forms a star formation as they descend over the Coronado Bay Bridge and NAB Coronado. Both SEAL parachuting demonstrations occurred in different years but on the same Fourth of July demonstration.

A squad of SEALs inserts ashore from the NSW RIBs onto the beach by the Coronado golf course during a Fourth of July NSW demonstration.

Another squad of SEALs files off the bow of the MSSC and inserts onto the Coronado boat ramp during a Fourth of July demonstration. The MSSC above is a Vietnam-era SEAL support boat. (Author's collection.)

The pilot and navigator of the MK-8 Mod-0 SDV, with a 4-foot-tall shark fin on top of the boat, drive the SDV on the surface past enthusiastic boat parties to the demonstration site, where the SDV will mimic a man-eating shark versus a SEAL in the water. The SDV drives under the SEAL on the surface, and the navigator grabs the SEAL and pulls him underwater, appearing that the shark had eaten the SEAL. Later the SEAL appears on the surface victoriously holding the shark fin. (Both, author's collection.)

Actor Cliff Robertson sits in the back of the SDV as pilot Albert Shaufelberger and navigator Doc Wheeler drive the SDV over to the Coronado boat ramp, where the actor will disembark and join the *Mike Douglas Show* filming during a Fourth of July demonstration in Coronado. Lt. Cdr. Albert Shaufelberger later served as a U.S. Military Group advisor and was assassinated in El Salvador in 1983. (Author's collection.)

The Creature from the Black Lagoon rides in the older MK-7 SDV as the pilot drives the SDV around for the Coronado Fourth of July demonstration audience. A full life-size model of the Creature sits at the entrance to the BUD/S training building.

Above, Super Frog contestants run in wet suits down the Coronado beach to enter back into water to commence the second swim circuit before the bike-racing leg of the competition. Volunteer BUD/S students clap and encourage the competitors. Below, Moki Martin, retired SEAL and Super Frog leader, makes opening comments to the crowd and competitors before they start the competition, located just behind the SEAL team area on the Silver Strand, Coronado, California. (Both, author's collection.)

Navy SEALs line up in the first row ready to participate in the Coronado half-marathon that used to run throughout Coronado and onto North Island Naval Air Station. The half-marathon was run in the early morning before the Coronado parade. (Author's collection.)

SEALs jump out of the back of a CH-53 helicopter to their CRRC below during a demonstration of SEAL helicopter cast and recovery tactics. (Author's collection.)

The Leap Frogs jump team demonstrates a difficult maneuver with their parachutes before landing onto the landing zone at the 2008 UDT/SEAL reunion in Coronado, California. (Author's collection.)

Lou De Lara and William Giannotti emplace a half-pound demolition charge onto the metal rebar protrusions of this cement tanker, the gambling ship *Monte Carlo* that washed ashore after a storm in 1936 onto the beach near the Hotel Del Coronado. UDT-1 conducted the demolition of the wreckage with small demo charges at the request of the City of Coronado but without causing disruption to the surrounding community. (Courtesy L. De Lara.)

Navy SEAL dependants Joyce (center) and Catherine Wood (right) and DDS diver Guy Guiliani enjoy the Dependents Day Cruise standing crammed up in the control tower with the commanding officer of the USS *Kamehameha* in the Pacific Ocean. Community relations are beneficial to NSW dependants as well. (Author's collection.)

During many NSW demonstrations and sponsored SEAL pup days, SEALs will help demonstrate various NSW equipment and arms to children and young adults. SEAL dependant Amy Wood receives instruction on the M4 carbine. (Author's collection.)

Chief Michael Thornton, Medal of Honor winner, leads the SEAL and UDT floats in a Columbus Day parade in downtown San Diego as many San Diego residents look on.

Rear Adm. Garry Bonelli speaks to a crowd of local Coronado residents and retired and active duty SEALs and Frogs during the annual UDT/SEAL reunion held in Coronado, California. (Author's collection.)

NBC war correspondent George Folster (left) interviews UDT Frogmen after operations at Wonson Harbor, Korea, in October 1950.

Project Quick Find sea lion Aikahi, on a dressing stand, gives actor Cliff Robertson a kiss on the cheek as Mike Douglas interviews Lt. Don Ridgeway, Quick Find officer in charge, and Mike Kelley, the trainer holding Aikahi's harness. (Author's collection.)

Marlin Perkins, star of the
Mutual of Omaha television
show *Wild Kingdom*, gives
Aikahi a smelt reward as
Aikahi's trainer Dan Peterson
looks on. (Author's collection.)

Actor Richard Widmark, star of
the movie *The Frogmen*, talks
with Lt. Cdr. Kelley Welch,
a Korea War–era Frogman,
before the Widmark Studios
free movie presentation
to UDT personnel.

Providing tours of NSW commands and equipment to military and civilian dignitaries is a common occurrence, but some tours are a little off the beaten path. Above, author Michael Wood takes the assistant secretary of defense–Special Operations and Low Intensity Conflicts on a submerged tour in a MK-8 Mod-0 SDV in Glorietta Bay near the Coronado Bay Bridge. Below, Michael Wood takes civilian and military dignitaries on a tour of the Dry Deck Shelter (DDS), a deep submergence system that attaches to the deck of a selected submarine and houses the SDV or other NSW operational personnel and equipment. (Both, author's collection.)

# Seven

# THE AREA

"The area" is a term used by team guys referring to the home base command area where they are currently assigned. These "areas" can become like a second home depending on the length of time of the Frog or SEAL tour. For SEALs of San Diego, "the area" will mean their home base is located at the SEAL Team compounds or the BUD/S training compound on the Silver Strand in Coronado, California. Other NSW groups and commands are stationed throughout the area on the ocean and bay sides of the base.

Depending on the time frame, some of these NSW commands have changed location and appearance, with some commands moving away to Hawaii and a bunch of new commands starting up on the Naval Amphibious Base in Coronado. Cdr. Draper Kauffman was instrumental in setting up the first UDT facility at the new Naval Amphibious Base that started in tents. From that day after World War II until now, the presence of NSW has expanded manyfold to the extent that today NSW occupies close to 30 percent of the base, including NSWC headquarters; NAVSPECWARCEN, which includes BUD/S; NSWG-1, NSWG-3, and NSWG-11; Special Boat Team TWELVE; ST-1, ST-3, ST-5, and ST-7; and Support Activity ONE.

Other areas where SEALs of San Diego spend a good deal of time are the training areas at Niland and San Clemente Island (SCI), California. Both these areas have been used by UDT and SEALs for at least the last 40 years, mainly for BUD/S training and SEAL platoons' advanced training. The Niland Chocolate Mountains have been the site of many training patrols, live fire and demolition maneuvers, small unit tactics, and weapons firing of every type. San Clemente rock shores and cliffs and cold deep waters have been the locations for small unit tactics, weapons, and demolition training but also include diving training, underwater demolitions, and hydrographic reconnaissance.

This is a 1949 aerial view of the ATB Coronado showing the San Diego Bay side of the base on the left and the Silver Strand ocean side on the right with the UDT compound in the lower right

This photograph shows the UDT headquarters, training, maintenance, and berthing Quonset huts of the post–World War II era on ATB Coronado along the Silver Strand beach.

corner of the photograph. Cdr. Draper Kauffman was instrumental in setting up a UDT facility at the new Naval Amphibious Base.

PN3 Ken Garret, UDT-1, is standing in front of the sign at the entrance to the UDT compound. Garret's attire reflects the poor logistical support that existed in this time period. He is wearing army shoes, Seabee trousers, a Marine Corps shirt with USMC logo, and has a hat from the army.

In 1949, the coast off of the Silver Strand in Coronado, California, was the site of large-scale amphibious landing operations, with UDT Frogmen placing training explosives on beach obstacles exposed in the surf zone.

This is a more current view of the Silver Strand beach behind the SEAL team areas looking toward the Coronado high-rises. BUD/S student boat crews run down the beach with IBS on their heads during one of their many Hell Week evolutions.

A more current-day view of NAB Coronado clearly shows on the left beach side the Commander NSW headquarters. In the middle beach area are the ST-1, ST-3, ST-5, and ST-7 compounds, and to the right are the BUD/S training compound and obstacle course. On the bay side or main base is NSWG-1 headquarters just inside the main gate to the left, and on the other end of the base by the piers is NSWG-3 headquarters and Special Boat Team TWELVE.

ATB Coronado, California, in 1943 is in the early stages of being constructed and showing the landfill.

## Underwater Demolition Training at San Clemente

EXPLOSION RESULT—Lieutenant M. M. Parker, Senior Instructor of Underwater Demolition Training, right, points out the results of an explosive charge which had been placed on a railroad rail. The rail had been cut in two, and pieces scattered in a wide area. Trainees are, left to right, Ensign John F. Callahan, R. W. Belote, SN; L. M. Cifuentes, BM2; and R. R. Ruecheim, FA.

TRAINING CAMP-SITE—Underwater Demolition Training's "tent city" on China Point, San Clemente Island. This is the training headquarters from which night problems, demolition exercises and general training is conducted.

This newspaper article shows the SCI training camp, which began as a "tent city" with one Quonset hut as the main structure at the Northwest Cove area. (Courtesy W. Otte.)

The early days of the BUD/S camp changed to trailers with a view of the water tower up on the hill, which the students run up for their flight of the wooden butterfly. Later metal Butler buildings were constructed to house BUD/S students, instructors, and visiting UDT/SEAL platoons. Tents to trailers to Butler buildings and finally new BUD/S facilities at Northwest Harbor were completed, including 23 new buildings.

Niland, California, became a popular SEAL/UDT land warfare training area for both BUD/S and SEAL advanced training. Initially, training was conducted with no facilities, operating from trucks and living in a trailer behind Scotty's gas station at Niland. Later old MWR (Morale, Welfare, Recreation) trailers were moved in as makeshift shelters. At right is P. K. Barnes near a trailer as his ST-1 X-ray platoon conducts Niland advanced operator training. (Courtesy D. Peterson.)

The Butler buildings constructed at Niland served as the next home for BUD/S and UDT/SEAL units. The Butler buildings were metal, and the desert coolers provided some cooling comfort from the heat. The back of one of the buildings shows the desert coolers and the weapons cleaning station. (Courtesy R. Kelley.)

# Frogmen 'Move Up' From Quonsets

## $575,000 Unit Houses Navy Teams

### By JOHN BUNKER

Navy frogmen at the Coronado Amphibious Base have exchanged wartime quonset huts for a $570,000 headquarters along the Coronado Silver Strand.

The new headquarters is "home port" for Underwater Demolition Unit 1, which sends teams of swimmers on acquatic missions all over the Pacific — from the frigid fringes of the Beaufort Sea to coral shores of the South Pacific.

These men of the sea are only a running jump from high-water mark. The Coronado sands are their daily parade ground and their drill field is the blue Pacific, less than a hundred yards beyond their back door.

The new facility was constructed to give the Pacific Fleet's underwater demolition teams 11 and 12 a base in keeping with their increasing importance to fleet activities.

Constructed in the form of a quadrangle, it contains offices, classrooms, shops, armories, and storage spaces.

Each team has its own armory, diving locker, storerooms, carpenter shop, and electronics shop. Stored and repaired in the armories are the small and compact but highly lethal weapons of these underwater warriors: machine guns, knives, and demolition equipment.

In the diving lockers are aqualungs, depth gauges, waterproof watches and other gear carried by these submarine scouts in operations against enemy beach defenses or in sub-sea explorations and charting work.

One of the most important features of the new UDU base is a full-size decompression chamber such as those used on submarine rescue ships to handle cases of divers' bends. Bends is caused by the accumulation of nitrogen bubbles in the blood stream when divers ascend too rapidly from deep water. Decompression chambers provide the air pressure a diver would experience in deep water and counteracts effects from the bends if the diver reaches it soon enough after coming out of the water.

The decompression chamber also is used to test new recruits in underwater work and determine their ability to breathe oxygen for prolonged periods.

Another important installation in this new facility is a big compressor room, where aqua lungs are charged with high-pressure air.

The quadrangle provides space for physical conditioning exercises and a helicopter deck where aircraft can land with divers being rushed to the decompression chamber.

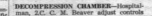

**DECOMPRESSION CHAMBER**—Hospitalman, 2.C. C. M. Beaver adjust controls on the decompression chamber while Hospitalman, 2.C., Joseph Barber emerges. At right, Barber checks Beaver's oxygen mask before making a test run.

A San Diego news article announced the completion of the new UDU-1 building on the Silver Strand in Coronado, California, to house UDT-11 and UDT-12. This allowed the UDTs to move out of the World War II Quonset huts into more up-to-date facilities, including a new recompression chamber in case of diving accidents. (Courtesy W. Otte.)

Author Michael Wood, wearing twin 90-cubic-foot scuba bottles and double hose regulator, walks back to the third-phase dive locker at the old BUD/S training area on the bay side of NAB Coronado. During this time period, third phase was the diving phase instead of the land warfare phase. This BUD/S training area was still using buildings left over from the post–World War II and Korean War eras. (Author's collection.)

# *Eight*

# HONORS AND ACCOMPLISHMENTS

This honor roll chapter is meant to provide only a small peek at the numerous honors and accomplishments achieved by the Frogs and SEALs of San Diego. The honors are represented by the military awards presented to individuals and entire teams, as well as honors and achievements that extend well beyond just military awards. The accomplishments mentioned are also a small sampling and represent only the military-related accomplishments. Many Frogs and SEALs have gone on to a wide variety of accomplishments outside of the military, including commercial and corporate achievements, academic and sports achievements, community service, state and local government, law enforcement, political positions in the House of Representatives and Senate, and achievements in the scientific and medical communities. There appear to be no restrictions to how far Frogs and SEALs will employ their military skills and abilities and apply them to accomplishments that continue to serve their families, friends, communities, home states, God, and country.

Some of these achievements not covered in the photographs and captions to follow include a wide variety of arenas of life. The political arena includes former ST-1 member Robert Kerrey, former Democratic governor of Nebraska from 1983 to 1987 and a U.S. senator from Nebraska (1989–2001). Another politician of note was former UDT member Jesse Ventura (born James George Janos), formerly a professional wrestler, movie actor, and governor of Minnesota from January 4, 1999, to January 6, 2003. There are several West Coast ST-1 members who went on to become preachers or missionaries of various Christian denominations, such as Woody Shoemaker, Dan Cergoni, and Sam Birky. In the corporate and commercial arena, there is Blackwater president Gary Jackson, from a SEAL team. Maybe not as famous is local owner of McP's Irish Pub and Grill and author of the book *Combat Corpsman* Greg McPartlin, a former member of ST-1 and UDT. These are just a few who have employed their SEAL skills to accomplish achievements in other areas of life.

A legend, his name is etched forever on the NAVSPECWARCEN, NAB Coronado, California. Then ensign Phil Bucklew earned a Silver Star as a Scout and Raider on a kayak reconnaissance mission under heavy fire off Green Beach, Salerno, in September 1943. He is one of the first 10 volunteers for a new unit, the Amphibious Scouts and Raiders. His World War II exploits took him to North Africa, Gibraltar, Casablanca, Sicily, Omaha Beach, and later China. In 1955, Lt. Cdr. Bucklew was assigned to a Naval Advisory Group in Korea operated from a clandestine base off Inchon, conducting agent infiltration, harassment, and psychological operations against North Korea. Later as Commander Amphibious Group ONE, he helped supervise beach reconnaissance of South Vietnam using an assigned UDT-12 detachment. Later he became executive officer of NAB Coronado and then commander of the new Naval Operations Support Group Pacific, commanding all SEALs, UDTs, Beach Jumpers, and Boat Units. Pictured below is Bucklew, the "father of NSW."

Lt. (jg) J. Robert "Bob" Kerrey receives the Medal of Honor (MOH) from Pres. Richard Nixon as family and friends observe. He received the MOH for conspicuous gallantry when he led his SEAL platoon to capture an important Vietcong political cadre located on an island in the bay of Nha Trang. Though seriously wounded, he and his SEAL platoon successfully completed the mission despite intense enemy resistance. Bob Kerry later became the Democratic governor and senator of Nebraska. Below, Bob Kerry (left) sits with a shipmate on a MSSC.

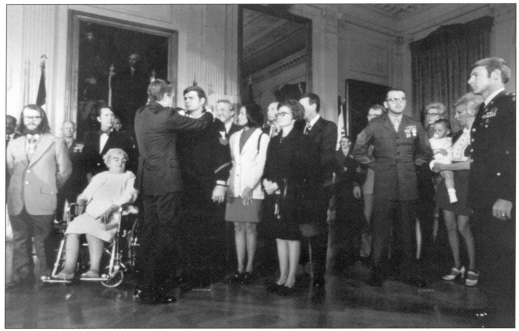

Michael Thornton receives the Medal of Honor from Pres. Richard Nixon as family and friends look on. Engineman Second Class Thornton was awarded for action as a navy SEAL on an intelligence gathering and prisoner capture operation with Lt. Tom Norris and a three-man Vietnamese patrol. The patrol came into heavy fire from numerically superior forces, engaged in a fierce firefight, and moved back. Thornton, upon learning the senior officer was hit and believed dead by enemy fire, returned into the hail of fire, killing several enemy, recovering his lieutenant's lifeless body, and swimming several hours out to sea, where all in the patrol were successfully recovered.

Lt. Michael Murphy (29), from SDVT-1, received a posthumous Medal of Honor for actions in battle in Iraq and Afghanistan. He was killed during a reconnaissance mission in Afghanistan while leading a four-man team looking for a key Taliban leader in mountainous terrain near Asadabad. While in their sniper hideout, the team came under heavy fire from a much larger enemy force, and though mortally wounded, Murphy knowingly exposed himself to get a clear communications signal to call in support for his team. He then returned to his cover and the fight until succumbing to his wounds.

PO2 Michael Monsoor from ST-3 received a posthumous Medal of Honor for actions in battle in Iraq. Monsoor was on a sniper detail with three other SEALs in Ar Ramadi, Iraq, when an insurgent threw a fragmentation grenade into their building hide site. The grenade hit Monsoor on the chest, then it dropped to the ground. Positioned next to the single exit, Monsoor was the only one who could have escaped harm. Instead, he dropped onto the grenade to shield the others from the blast.

In 1969, ST-1 members in front of the White House include, from left to right, (kneeling) Pete Slempa, Claude Willis, Frank Flynn, Doc Jones, Bill Garnet, Kenney Estock, and Clarence Betts; (standing) Dave Schiably, Jack Schropp, Chuck Lemoyn, Harold Mathews, Bob Sell, Robert Kelly, Ron Ostrander, Tom Macdonald, Frank Bomar, Moki Martin, Guy Stone, Ron Bell, and Frank Anderson. These men received the Presidential Unit Citation, or PUC, which is awarded to a unit, not an individual.

Officers and men of ST-1 receive the PUC from Pres. Lyndon Johnson in the White House West Room. From left to right are (first row) Guy Stone, Ron Bell, Dave Sitter, Wayne Jones, Clarence Betts, unidentified, President Johnson, Dave Schiably, and Frank Anderson; (second row) Bill Garnet, two unidentified, Robert Kelly, Joe Defloria, two unidentified, Ron Ostrander, Moki Martin, Jack Schropp, Chuck Lemoyne, and unidentified.

Rear Adm. Joseph Kernan, commander of NSWC, presents a navy and Marine Corps achievement medal to Moki Martin, resident of Coronado, California, for heroic service during Operation Thunderhead, a recently revealed secret mission during the Vietnam War to rescue escaped American POWs. The POW escape did not occur as planned, unknown to the rescue team, but the team was launched from a submarine and used a swimmer delivery vehicle for infiltration during Operation Thunderhead.

A few Operation Thunderhead members of the ST-1 Alfa platoon gather at McP's Irish Pub and Grill following the award ceremony held at NSWC. From left to right are (first row) Lt. Cdr. Edward Towers (Ret.), Moki Martin, and Frank Sales; (second row) Bob Hook, Rick Hetzel, and Tim Reeves. The mural on the McP's wall in the background is the famous Freddie the Frog caricature painted by local former SEAL Pete "the Pirate" Carolyn. McP's is a popular SEAL hangout and is owned by former navy SEAL Greg McPartlin. (Author's collection.)

Family members and friends of fallen Navy SEALs watch as the Pacific Beacon unaccompanied personnel housing is unveiled during a dedication ceremony in San Diego. The buildings were named in honor of three SEALs: Sonar Technician (Surface) Second Class (SEAL) Matthew Axelson and Gunner's Mate Second Class (SEAL) Danny Dietz, who were killed during Operation Redwings in Afghanistan on June 28, 2005, and Interior Communications Electrician First Class (SEAL) Thomas Retzer, who was killed in Afghanistan on June 25, 2003, while supporting Operation Enduring Freedom.

Capt. Everett L. Greene became the first NSW commissioned black officer when he completed BUD/S training in 1971 as an ensign. Operationally, he has served in a ST-1 platoon; as plans officer with NSWG-1 Detachment WESTPAC and Joint Special Operations Command (JSOC); executive officer of NSW Unit ONE; commanding officer of Special Boat Unit TWELVE; and ultimately as the first commander of Special Boat Squadron ONE, a major NSW command at NAB Coronado. (Courtesy NSWG-3.)

Tiz Morrison (right) stands in trunks with swim fins next to James Gilmore at a presumed location of UDT training at Maui in 1945. Morrison is credited with being the first black Frogman, in 1945, and UDT instructor, in 1949. He volunteered for UDT duty as a line seaman in 1945 and was one of six who graduated from the 115-man training class. He was titled "King of the Frogmen" by a magazine article, and teammates would not let the regal title die. His reputation was well earned as a battle-tested veteran of Korea who served 19 years in UDT-1, UDT-12, and UDT training, having deployed to Japan, China, Korea, Greece, Cuba, Italy, and Pakistan. He retired in 1962. Tiz was a longtime resident of the San Diego County area. Below are Korean War medal recipients: (first row) Al Bass, Tim Frazier, Tiz Morrison, Mack Boynton, and C. H. Boswell; (second row) Lt. Cdr. Kelley Welch (commanding officer of UDT-1), Lt. (jg) K. J. Christoph, Capt. Selden Small (commanding officer of Amphibious Group ONE ), and Lt. Ted Fielding (executive officer of UDT-1). (Both, courtesy UDT-SEAL Museum.)

This is a portrait of Adm. Eric T. Olson in his camouflage uniform as a four-star admiral and commander of U.S. Special Operations Command (USSOCOM). Admiral Olson is the first NSW officer to become a three-star and four-star admiral and the first navy SEAL to become the USSOCOM combatant commander. His combat and wartime history include the battle of Mogadishu, commander of NSW Task Unit Sierra during Desert Storm, and service in Israel, Egypt, and Tunisia. Below, Adm. Eric T. Olson is congratulated by Secretary of Defense Robert Gates and outgoing USSOCOM commander army general Doug Brown during the USSOCOM change of command ceremony.

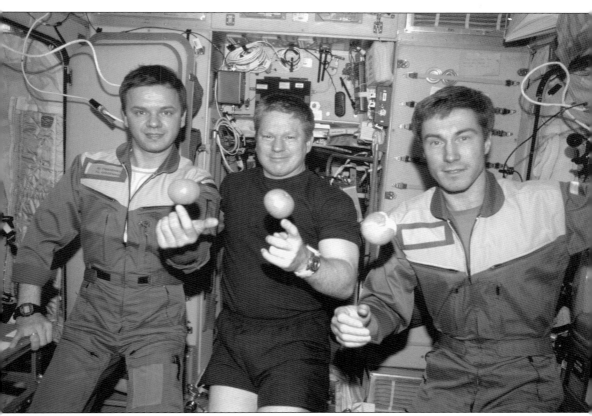

The Expedition One crew members are about to eat fresh oranges onboard Zvezda Service Module of the Earth-orbiting International Space Station (ISS) in space from October 31, 2000, to March 21, 2001. From left to right are cosmonaut Yuri Gidzenko, Soyuz commander; astronaut William Shepherd, mission commander; and cosmonaut Sergei Krikalev, flight engineer. From Frogman to spaceman, Astro-Frog William M. Shepherd (captain, U.S. Navy) graduated from the U.S. Naval Academy in 1971 and served as a Frogman and SEAL member in San Diego in UDT-11 and ST-1 and later as a department head at NSWC headquarters. Selected by NASA in May 1984, Shepherd is a veteran of four space flights, logging over 159 days in space. Earlier, he made three flights as a mission specialist on STS-27, STS-41, and STS-52 from 1988 to 1992. Shepherd is currently serving as a science advisor for USSOCOM. His job application for this position was sent by text message from the Space Station to his current boss, Adm. Eric Olson, commander of USSOCOM. (Courtesy NASA.)

Fourth from right standing is Cathal "Irish" Flynn, later to become the first "active duty" navy SEAL officer promoted to Flag rank as rear admiral in 1985. A *Life* magazine reporter took this photograph of ST-1 Alfa platoon, a Special Boat Unit (SBU) crewman, and interpreter on the Bassac River near Binh Thuy in late 1967. Lieutenant Flynn was Detachment Golf's officer in command, based at Nha Be, Vietnam. In 1983, Flynn led the conversion of all four UDTs to SEAL teams. Alfa platoon members are, from left to right, (first row) two unidentified, RM2 Ron Byrum, EN3 Mitch Bucklew, SK2 Walter "Apo" Gouveia, and Lt. Joe Defloria, platoon commander; (second row) PO3 Richard Williams, Lt. Cathal Flynn, MM1 Moki Martin, and AK2 Ron Ostrander. (Courtesy M. Martin.)

Vice Adm. Joseph Kernan is the first navy SEAL to be assigned as a navy fleet commander. Vice Admiral Kernan will serve both as commander of the U.S. 4th Fleet and commander for U.S. Naval Forces Southern Command in Mayport, Florida. U.S. 4th Fleet is responsible for navy ships, aircraft, and submarines operating in the Caribbean Sea and Central and South America.

Chief Gunners Mate Barry Enoch, to this author's knowledge, has no "firsts," does not have a Medal of Honor, and has not achieved governor or senator status. What he is is a highly decorated warrior and the "Teammate" of teammates. He is a highly revered SEAL operator whose humble demeanor even survived authorship of his book, *Teammates–SEALs at War*, where he takes the reader on the mission, focusing not on himself but his teammates. Above, Barry Enoch takes care of a young Vietnamese child while out in the field with ST-1 Alfa platoon. (Courtesy C. Maury.)

Vice Adm. Albert M. Calland III (Ret.) has many accomplishments to his name, such as being a Naval Academy football record-setting wide receiver, but what is unique about his career is that he is the first SEAL to become the deputy director of the CIA, from July 2005 to July 2006. Vice Admiral Calland is a 1974 graduate of the Naval Academy and a 1975 graduate of BUD/S Class 82 training. Commands in San Diego that he has served are commander of NSWC, NSWG-1, commanding officer of ST-1, executive officer of Special Boat Team TWELVE, and SDV and SEAL platoon commander. He had been a longtime resident of the San Diego area.

Francis Douglas "Red Dog" Fane was a former surface warrior from 1940 to 1945, with World War II combat experience in the Aleutians, Sicily, Marshall Islands, Marianas, and New Guinea. Then Lt. (jg) Francis Fane volunteered for UDT and at 33 years old completed UDT training in 1945. Lieutenant Fane later commanded UDT-13 and was among the first U.S. forces to land in Japan. Lieutenant Fane is credited with fighting to keep UDT alive during the post–World War II period. He led UDT into the diving world, testing multiple closed and semi-closed diving rigs and diver transport vehicles leading to today's SDV teams. Soon after the Korean War started, Lieutenant Commander Fane was the senior UDT officer in Korea. He returned to San Diego, and later as commander, Fane commanded UDT-1 in Coronado. His enormous amount of accomplishments are too numerous to mention. He retired as a captain in 1960.

SEAL teammates bestow the final honor of being piped over the side and gonged ashore by ship's bell to Cdr. Michael Wood for his 34 years of service as enlisted man and commissioned officer, having served in Vietnam, Desert Storm, and Somalia as part of SEAL, UDT, and SDV teams. His wife, Joyce, joins him for the final piping over as a class of BUD/S students yells in the background over the berm in a deep resounding voice, "HOOYAH CDR WOOD," from just behind the NSWC headquarters on the beach in Coronado, California, in 2003. (Courtesy G. Anderson.)

At a recent funeral service for a fallen SEAL member, each attending SEAL walked up to the casket, removed the Trident from their uniform breast, and slammed the three sharp points of the warfare pin into the casket, deeply embedding it and leaving behind a little of themselves for their departing warrior, friend, and teammate. These embedded Tridents are representative of all the Frogs and SEALs, from World War II until today, who have given their life in the defense of their country. All total, there have been 168 Frogs and SEALs, both from the West and East Coasts, who have paid the ultimate price in combat for their family, friends, country, and God: World War II (85), Korea (2), Vietnam (48), Grenada (4), Panama (4), Kosovo (1), Afghanistan (17), and Iraq (7)—to date. To all those honored warriors, a big HOOYAH and God bless.

# DISCOVER THOUSANDS OF LOCAL HISTORY BOOKS FEATURING MILLIONS OF VINTAGE IMAGES

Arcadia Publishing, the leading local history publisher in the United States, is committed to making history accessible and meaningful through publishing books that celebrate and preserve the heritage of America's people and places.

Find more books like this at
**www.arcadiapublishing.com**

Search for your hometown history, your old stomping grounds, and even your favorite sports team.

MADE IN THE USA